FOLK SILVER ACCESSORIES

FOLK SILVER ACCESSORIES

Compiled by Wang Jinhua

FOREIGN LANGUAGES PRESS

First Edition 2008

ISBN 978-7-119-04676-1

Published by
Foreign Languages Press
24 Baiwanzhuang Road, Beijing 100037, China
http: //www. flp. com. cn

Distributed by
China International Book Trading Corporation
35 Chegongzhuang Xilu, Beijing 100044, China
P.O. Box 399, Beijing, China

Printed in the People's Republic of China

Contents

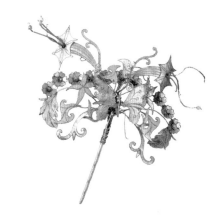

INTRODUCTION

Chinese silverware dates back to the 5th to the 3rd century BC, when many of China's unearthed silver accessories were produced, such as: the gilded silver buckle inlaid with jade and glaze found in Huixian County, Henan Province; the ape-shaped silver ornament unearthed in Qufu, Shandong Province; the nine pieces of silver accessories in a Hun (ancient Chinese nomadic people) tomb in Inner Mongolia; the silver tiger, deer and hoops in Shaanxi Province; and the more than 100 pieces of silverware in the tomb of Liu Xiang (?-179 BC, king of the State of Qi during the Western Han Dynasty). Among the silverware found in Liu Xiang's tomb were an engraved gold-plated silver plate and a small design-gilded silver plate produced in 214 BC. All of these serve as a testament to the superb silver-crafting skills during those times.

During the heyday of China's silver-crafting (7th-9th centuries), silverware was produced in large quantities with a wide diversity, and was widely distributed. It also featured exquisite and highly skilled designs.

Gold crown,
Warring States Period:
Inner Mongolia

Gilded bronze kettle carved
with a coiled dragon design,
Han Dynasty

Gold four-dragon bracelet,
Tang Dynasty:
Tang tomb in Xianyang

Imperial Maids with Hairpins, Tang Dynasty

From the 10th to the 14th century, silverware production became commercialized and the skills of casting, carving, engraving and welding were improved. Silver accessories, which earlier could only be used by royal and noble families and rich merchants, began to spread among the common people. They featured a wider variety and more lively designs. The designs covered the following themes: flowers, birds, fishes and insects; pavilions, chambers and towers; plants and other auspicious designs; and even lines of poetry.

The period from the 14th to the 20th century witnessed an unprecedented development in Chinese metal work. The gold and silver accessories and vessels became more diversified and luxurious. From 1426 to 1436, the Casting Bureau instituted a regulation that all regional craftsmen must work for the royal court for three months in the capital city, which greatly spurred the development of metal craft.

During this period, with the rapid development of metal craft, silverware workshops sprang up as a non-governmental industry. A great deal of small silverware of practical and aesthetic value emerged, such as silver cigarette cases, pipes, snuff bottles, rouge cases and incense burners, as the skills of polishing, engraving and carving achieved maturity.

Tibetan silver accessories:
Yushu, Qinghai Province

From the 17th to the 19th century, enamel silverware production thrived. And the first half of the 20th century saw the rapid development and large-scale production of folk silver accessories.

Tibetan women's accessories:
Yushu, Qinghai Province

Miao hat ornaments: Guizhou

Miao silver necklace: Leishan, Guizhou

Miao silver lock: Leishan, Guizhou

Tibetan waist ornaments: Yushu, Qinghai

Introduction

Miao silver accessories: Leishan, Guizhou

HEADWEAR

Headwear

Silver headwear refers to elegant silver crowns worn by noble families.

Gilded silver headwear with endless
knots and vines and coral, Mongolian style,
late Qing Dynasty

Endless Knot

The "Endless Knot" is one of the eight Buddhist treasures (the other seven being: Wheel, Conch Shell, Parasol, Victory Banner, Lotus, Treasure Vase, and Pair of Gold Fish). The Knot is a long twisted rope, which symbolizes endless Buddhist blessings. It is widely used as an auspicious symbol on windows, balustrades, buttons, hairpins, etc.

Winding Vine

The design of "Winding Vine," also called "Winding Grass" or "Longevity Vine", dates back to the early 3rd century and has been popular ever since. This pattern features curving vines with flowers, buds, leaves and fruits on them, representing different growth periods of plants; therefore, the pattern is used to symbolize endless life or posterity.

Gilded silver crown (profile)

Coiled vine-design silver crown inlaid with coral,
Mongolian style, Republic of China

Detail of a silver crown

Gilded silver crown with coral and endless knots and vines (back),
Mongolian style, late Qing Dynasty

HAIR ACCESSORIES

Hair Accessories

In ancient times, Chinese women did up their hair in a bun, which they fixed with hair accessories. Such hair accessories included *zan*, *chai*, *buyao*, *bianfang* and combs.

Butterfly *zan*, Qing Dynasty

Zan

Ancient Chinese men and women both wore their hair long and got their hair or crowns fixed with *zan*, an ornamental long single-point hairpin. The earliest *zan* appeared in the Neolithic Age. During the 17th and the 3rd centuries BC, *zan* was usually made of bones; not until the 2nd century BC to the 3rd century AD were ivory, jade and turquoise used; from the 7th to the 14th century, expensive materials such as gold and silver were adopted.

Carving, hollowing, knotting and weaving were commonly used skills to make silver *zan*. And the designs were varied, for instance, in the form of plants, animals and vessels or geometric shapes. And they were generally auspiciously symbolic.

Gilded butterfly-and-flower *zan*,
Qing Dynasty

Gilded butterfly *zan*,
Qing Dynasty

Butterfly and Flower

Butterflies are considered an auspicious symbol. The butterfly-and-flower design indicates sweet love and a happy marriage.

Flower *zan*, Qing Dynasty

Butterfly-and-flower *zan*,
Qing Dynasty

Diancui zan, Qing Dynasty

Butterfly enamel *zan*, Qing Dynasty

God of Longevity

Since the 11th century BC, China began to worship the God of Longevity. From the 1st to the 3rd century, worshipping the God of Longevity was elevated to a national event, but this tradition was abolished during the 14th and the 17th centuries. The God of Longevity was originally a deity overseeing state stability and prosperity; and it was later worshipped as the deity responsible for people's lifespan. It has a unique appearance: a long face, big ears and a short body, holding a glossy ganoderma.

Enamel silver *zan* with designs of a butterfly and lobsters (left)
and the God of Longevity, Qing Dynasty

Enamel *zan* with a flower design,
Republic of China

God of Longevity *zan*,
Republic of China

Eight Immortals *zan*,
Republic of China

Bianfang

Another kind of hairpin, *bianfang* is shaped like a long tabular stick. Also called "Big Hairpin," it was originally used by Manchu women.

Coral-inlaid *bianfang* set (five pieces),
Mongolian style, Republic of China

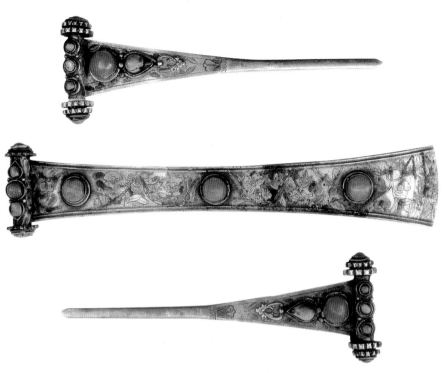

Coral-inlaid *bianfang*, Mongolian style,
Republic of China

Hair Accessories

Chinese Character 寿

The character 寿 (longevity) has different variants: long, narrow or round, each carrying a specific auspicious meaning. The combination of the Chinese characters for "10,000" and "longevity," *wanshou* in seal script refers to eternal life.

Gilded *bianfang* with the character 寿, early Republic of China

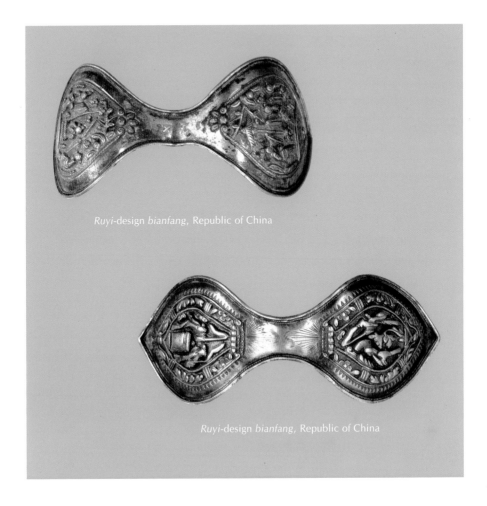

Ruyi

Ruyi means "as wished." In ancient China, there were four items that could be called *ruyi*: itch scratcher; auspicious paintings or instruments hung on the wall to dispel the evil; a tool with two cloud-design ends for Buddhist rituals and ceremonies; and auspicious imperial scepter.

The fourth became a popular gift among imperial family members after the 18th century, and the pattern was widely used in folk arts. It is shaped like an S, with one end in the shape of clouds or glossy ganoderma to signify good fortune as one wishes.

Ruyi-design *bianfang*, Republic of China

Ruyi-design *bianfang*, Republic of China

Chai

Chai is a two-prong hairpin to fix the hair in place. The procedure to make it is as follows: first, the two ends of a silver stick are hammered to a point, and bent in the middle; then the bent point is hammered into a geometric pattern, or twisted or welded into a ornamental design of flowers, animals or human figures; and it can then be inlaid with coral and agate. Molding, carving, cutting and engraving are adopted to make various designs and shapes.

Round flower-design enamel *chai*,
Qing Dynasty

Katydid-and-flower *diancui chai*,
Qing Dynasty

Katydids

Katydids are considered an auspicious insect. As the pronunciation of the Chinese name for katydid sounds similar to 哥 (elder brother), it indicates the wish for more baby boys. As the pronunciation also sounds similar to that of the word 官 (official) and katydids are good at jumping, they also symbolize leapfrog-like promotion.

Eight Hidden Treasures

"Eight Hidden Treasures" refer to the Eight Immortals' eight precious articles. They are Han Zhongli's banana-leaf fan, Zhang Guolao's fisherman's drum, Han Xiangzi's jade flute, Li Tieguai's magic gourd, Lü Dongbing's magic sword, Cao Guojiu's jade board, Lan Caihe's flower basket, and He Xiangu's lotus blossom. It is said that each of the eight treasures has a unique magical use. The Chinese people keep them as amulets in hopes of winning the Eight Immortals to their side.

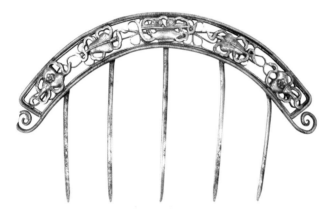

Chai with designs of the Eight Hidden Treasures, Qing Dynasty

Gilded lotus-design *chai*, Qing Dynasty

Lotus Design

The lotus was used as decoration as early as the 8th to the 3rd centuries BC. And it has been a Buddhist symbol since Buddhism was introduced in China. It represents pure land and good fortune.

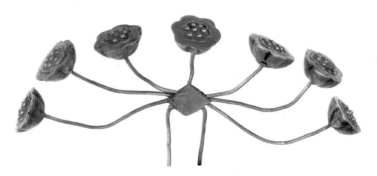

Gilded lotus-seedpod *chai*, Qing Dynasty: Shandong Province

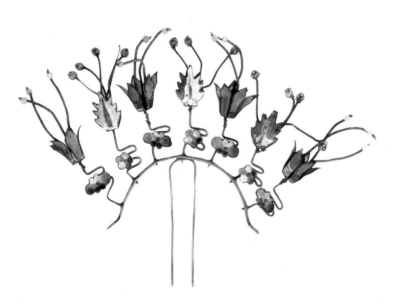

Enamel magnolia-design *chai*, Qing Dynasty

Safe in All Four Seasons

The Chinese character 瓶 (bottle) is a homophone (*ping*) of 平 (peace/safety). This design, composed of a bottle and four flowers representing the four seasons, signifies a smooth and safe year. The four flowers can be plum blossom, peony, lotus and chrysanthemum; or daffodil, lotus, chrysanthemum and plum blossom.

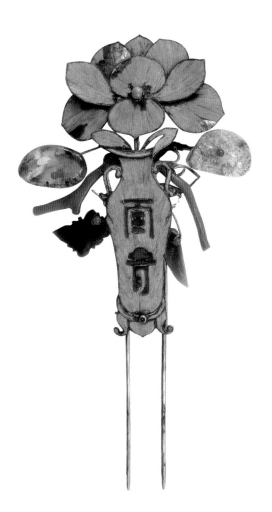
Chai for safety in all four seasons, Qing Dynasty

Three-plentiful Design

This design is composed of pomegranate, peach and chayote. The peach symbolizes longevity, the chayote represents happiness, and the pomegranate is a sign of fruitful posterity because of its large number of seeds. These three fruits come together to express good wishes for extra happiness, greater longevity and more children.

Three-plentiful-design *chai* with an ear-pick, Qing Dynasty

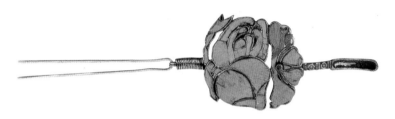

Cicada-design *chai* with an ear-pick, Qing Dynasty

Flower-design enamel *chai*, Qing Dynasty

Hair Accessories

Gilded deity-design
chai, Republic of China

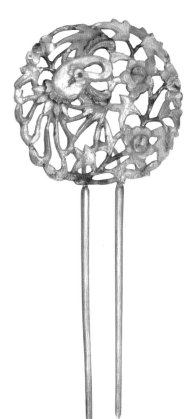

28

Flower-and-bird enamel *chai*,
early 20th century

Crab-design *chai* inlaid with agate,
Qing Dynasty

Wealth and Safety

Composed of a vase and peonies, this design signifies a harmonious and abundant life, as the peony symbolizes wealth and honor while the vase signifies safety.

Happiness and Longevity

This design is formed by peaches and bats or peaches and chayotes, or the two Chinese characters 福 (happiness) and 寿 (longevity). The peach symbolizes longevity, and the Chinese words for "bat" and "chayote" sound similar to that meaning "happiness."

Toad Design

It is said that Chang'e (the Moon Goddess) kept toads for company, and the legendary Liu Hai also had a gold three-legged toad. Therefore, the toad is thought of as a magic creature, signifying good fortune and wealth.

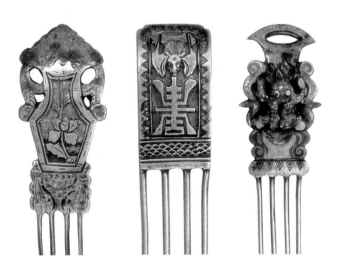

Chai with designs for wealth and safety (left), happiness and longevity (middle), and a gold toad (right), Qing Dynasty

Figure-design *chai*,
Qing Dynasty

Chai with designs for more
children and longer life and flowers,
Qing Dynasty

Crane-design enamel
chai with an ear-pick,
Qing Dynasty

Chai inlaid with jade,
kingfisher feathers and coral
beads, Qing Dynasty

Chayote-design enamel
chai with an ear-pick,
Qing Dynasty

Flower-and-leaf enamel
chai with an ear-pick,
Qing Dynasty

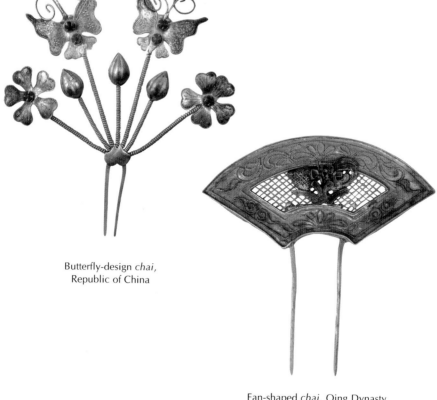

Butterfly-design *chai*,
Republic of China

Fan-shaped *chai*, Qing Dynasty

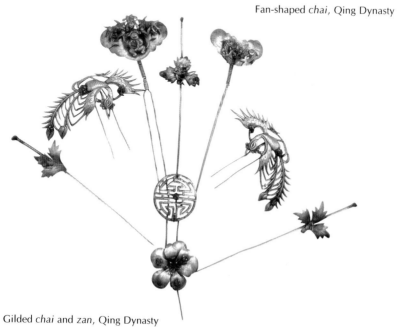

Gilded *chai* and *zan*, Qing Dynasty

Folk Silver Accessories

Chai and zan with flower,
butterfly and dragon designs,
Qing Dynasty

Enamel chai and zan, Qing Dynasty

Silver chai with a design for
more children and longer life,
Qing Dynasty

Zan with wires in
happiness-and-
longevity design and
with an ear-pick,
Republic of China

Chai and zan with bat and
flower designs and with an ear-pick,
Republic of China

Chai with
basket-and-bat
design and with
an ear-pick,
Qing Dynasty

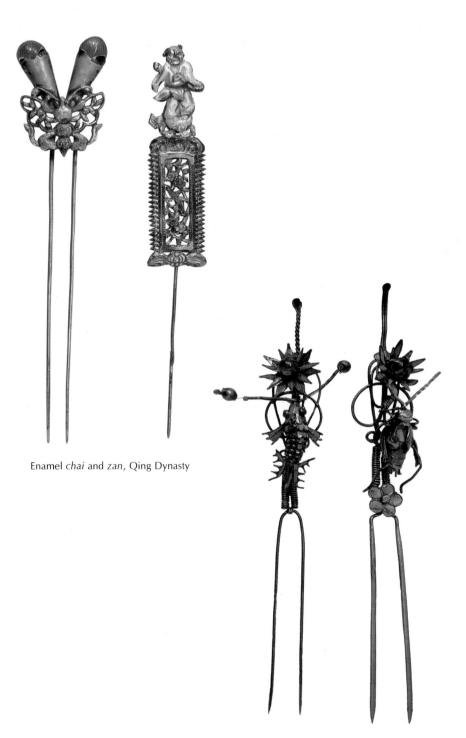

Enamel *chai* and *zan*, Qing Dynasty

Fish and katydid *chai* with an ear-pick,
Republic of China

Hair Accessories

Buyao

Buyao (dangling with each step) are ornaments attached to *zan* and *chai*. Rich in designs, *buyao* is made of strings of beads that dangle when the wearer is walking, hence its name. They first appeared in the 7th century BC, and became popular among noblewomen of the Han (206 BC-220) and Tang (618-907) dynasties.

Dragon-design *buyao*,
Qing Dynasty

Fan-shaped *buyao* with opera
characters, Qing Dynasty

Buyao with a jade
butterfly, Qing Dynasty

Buyao with the design of
zhuangyuan parading streets,
Republic of China

Zhuangyuan Parades the Streets

This design describes a scholar parading through the streets on horseback, after winning first place in the imperial examination. It signifies a smooth career.

Enamel *buyao* with figures and chrysanthemum, Qing Dynasty

Butterfly-and-flower *buyao* inlaid with jade,
late Qing Dynasty: Fujian

Butterfly-and-flower *buyao* inlaid with jade,
late Qing Dynasty: Fujian

Combs

In ancient China, combs were used not only to comb the hair and brush out dirt, but also to decorate the hair. Early in the Neolithic Age, combs made of bone appeared in China; followed by combs made from different materials, such as wood, bronze, gold and silver. Among them, wood and silver combs were the most common.

Silver comb with Chinese character 寿,
Qing Dynasty

Flower-design silver comb, Qing Dynasty

Silver comb with opera figures,
early 20th century: Jiangsu

Flower-design silver comb,
early 20th century: Hunan

Flower-design silver comb,
Republic of China

Folded silver comb,
Qing Dynasty

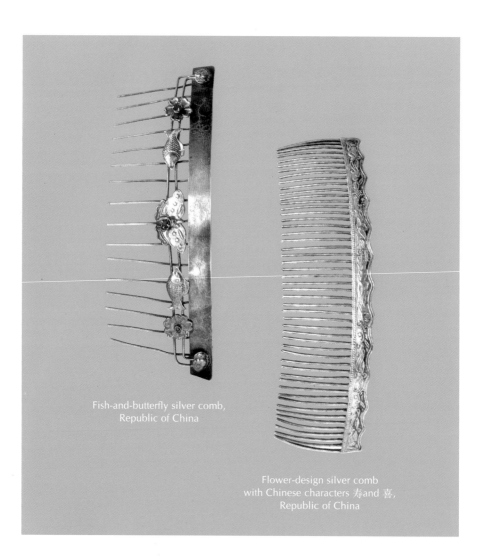

Fish-and-butterfly silver comb,
Republic of China

Flower-design silver comb
with Chinese characters 寿and 喜,
Republic of China

NECKLACES

Necklaces

Silver necklaces include torques and longevity locks.

Torques

Torques are usually made of bamboo, bronze, gold or silver, and are suitable for both men and women. From the 17th to the 20th century, silver torqueses were popular among Chinese youngsters. Today's Miao, Zhuang and Yao women still retain this tradition.

Blessing and Longevity

The design is often composed of bats and peaches, or chayotes and peaches. The first Chinese character in 蝙蝠 (bat) and 佛手 (chayote) sound similar to 福 (blessing), and the peach represents longevity. Or, simply put the two Chinese characters 福 (blessing) and 寿 (longevity) together to express good wishes.

Blessing-and-longevity torque, Republic of China

Blessing-and-longevity torque, Republic of China

Longevity Locks

Originally a custom south of the Yangtze River to keep away the evil, longevity locks became popular neck ornamentation for children after the Ming Dynasty (1368-1644). They were usually made of metal, particularly silver.

A longevity lock usually consists of two parts, a torque and a hanging lock. The torque is connected with the lock by a long chain, signifying a long life. "Lock" symbolizes to lock (protect) the child's life. The lock has various shapes, such as *ruyi*, butterfly and kylin (a legendary animal). The front side of the lock is carved with auspicious words, for example, "a long life and great fortune" (*chang ming fu gui*) or "five sons becoming officials" (*wu zi deng ke*).

Detail of the longevity lock with auspicious characters and lotuses

Two Dragons Playing with a Pearl

If there are more than two dragons, it is called "a group of dragons playing with a ball." It's said that dragons can spit out pearls, which can prevent floods and fires.

Necklaces

福祿壽桜椿

Lotus-design longevity lock with two dragons playing
with a pearl, early 20th century

Detail of the two dragons playing with a pearl

Butterfly-shaped longevity lock with children being taught, Qing Dynasty

Butterfly Design

Butterflies are considered an auspicious symbol, signifying a happy marriage and love. Moreover, the Chinese character 蝶 (butterfly) is a homophone (*die*) of 耋 (80 years old), therefore butterflies also have the meaning of long life.

Butterfly-shaped longevity lock with opera characters, Qing Dynasty

Detail of the butterfly-shaped longevity lock with opera characters

Double Happiness

This design, 囍, is composed of a pair of Chinese character 喜 (double happiness). It is very familiar to the Chinese people, and an indispensable auspicious symbol at Chinese weddings.

Five Sons Becoming Officials

This design is composed of five sons gathering in one room. It's said that once there was one man who came up with a great educational method, which helped all of his five sons obtain imperial degrees and become high-ranking officials. Such a design is mostly used on the wedding articles.

Longevity lock with the opera story of five sons becoming officials engraved on a 囍, Qing Dynasty

Longevity lock (detail)

Bogu Design

This design consists of a bronze burner, porcelain vase, *ruyi*, gold chime, books, paintings and calligraphy. Sometimes flowers and fruits are included too. *Bogu* design represents extensive knowledge and elegant demeanor. It was commonly used to decorate the homes of scholars and officials.

Bogu-design longevity lock
(front), early 20th century

Bogu-design longevity lock (back)

Butterfly-design longevity lock,
Qing Dynasty

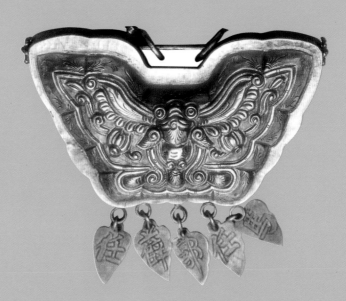

Detail of the butterfly-design longevity lock

Detail of the *bogu*-design longevity lock

Bogu-design longevity lock with Chinese characters meaning "happiness as boundless as the sea," Qing Dynasty

Kylin Delivering a Baby

This design depicts a kylin (Chinese unicorn) carrying a baby boy by riding clouds. The kylin is believed to be a benevolent animal, which brings people sons and heirs; and pious kylin believers could thus obtain sons. Benevolent and virtuous children who have literary talent are called "the toes of the kylin" or "kylin's sons."

Enamel longevity lock
with a kylin carrying a baby boy

Enamel longevity lock (front),
Republic of China

Longevity lock with a kylin carrying a boy,
early 20th century

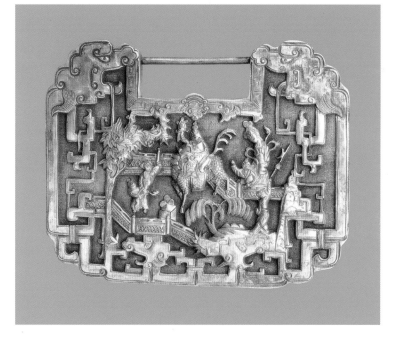

Longevity lock with the design of five sons becoming officials (back),
early 20th century

Longevity lock with a kylin carrying a boy,
Republic of China

Longevity lock with a kylin carrying a boy,
early 20th century

Longevity lock with a kylin carrying a boy

Necklaces

Baby-shaped longevity lock,
early 20th century

Longevity lock with auspicious design,
early 20th century

Gilded longevity lock with a kylin carrying a boy,
Qing Dynasty

Gilded longevity lock with a kylin carrying a boy,
Qing Dynasty

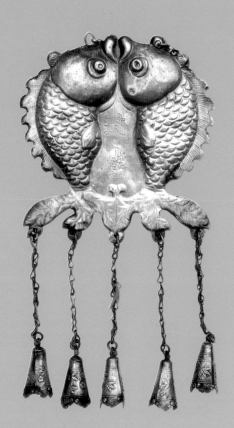

Surplus in Successive Years

This design is composed of children, carp and lotus. As 莲 (lotus) is a homophone (*lian*) of 连 (successive), and 鱼 (fish) is pronounced *yu* like 余 (surplus), when the two things, lotus and fish, are put together, it brings good wishes for surplus and a happy life every year.

Gilded longevity lock with a design of "surplus in successive years," Qing Dynasty

Longevity lock with design of "surplus in successive years," Qing Dynasty

Longevity lock with a boy riding a goat,
Qing Dynasty

One's House Filled with Gold and Jade

Since 鱼 (fish) and 玉 (jade) are homophonic (*yu*), goldfish (金鱼) is often used to represent gold and jade (金玉), or wealth in a broad sense. A house filled with gold and jade symbolizes wealth as well as talent.

Longevity lock of an auspicious goldfish,
Qing Dynasty

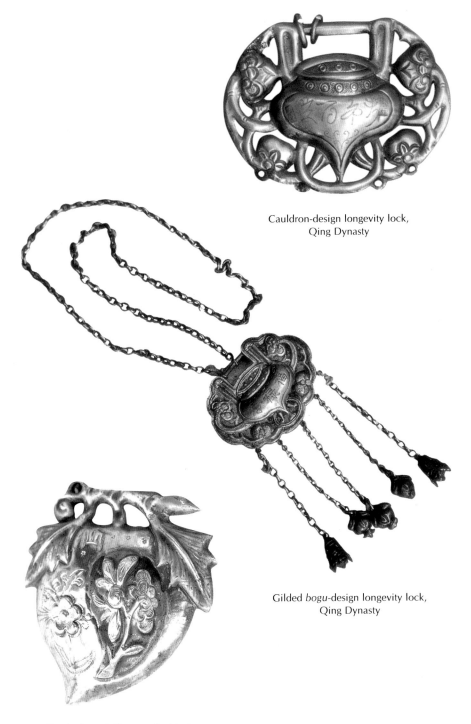

Cauldron-design longevity lock,
Qing Dynasty

Gilded *bogu*-design longevity lock,
Qing Dynasty

Peach-shaped silver pendant lock,
Republic of China: Shanxi

Liu Hai Playing with a Gold Toad

Liu Hai is a legendary figure. It's said that he often gives away money to make others rich; therefore, people often hang up pictures of him during festivals in the hopes of making more money. In the pictures, Liu Hai is depicted holding a string of gold coins while playing with a three-legged gold toad, an auspicious creature.

Longevity lock of Liu Hai playing with a gold toad, Qing Dynasty

Basket-shaped longevity lock, Qing Dynasty

Longevity lock of Liu Hai playing with a gold toad

If a longevity lock is carved with many family names, it signifies that all of these families are protecting the child.

Lotus-shaped 100-family-name longevity lock,
late Qing Dynasty: Hebei

Longevity lock with *zhuangyuan* riding
a horse, Qing Dynasty

Drum-shaped longevity lock,
early 20th century

Necklaces

Butterfly-shaped longevity lock,
Qing Dynasty

Silver-ingot-shaped longevity lock,
Qing Dynasty

Lion Playing with a Ball

This design is composed of lions and embroidered balls. Lions are considered the king of animals. They are so fierce and awesome-looking that the Chinese people believe they can dispel evil spirits and protect the family. Silk balls are also auspicious articles.

The Chinese characters 狮 (lion) and 师 (scholar) are homophonic (*shi*); while and 球 (ball) and 求 (seek) are both pronounced *Qiu*, therefore, this design symbolizes attaining official rank and power. It's said that if the fur of the female and male lions become tangled and rolled into a ball when they are playing together, the fur ball can transform into baby lions. This is why the design also signifies hopes for more progeny and a prosperous family. Derived from this design is the Lion Dance, which creates an auspicious atmosphere in Chinese cultural activities.

Longevity lock with two lions playing with a ball, Qing Dynasty

Cauldron-shaped longevity lock,
early 20th century

Gilded longevity lock with a pig design,
Qing Dynasty

Twelve Symbolic Zodiac Animals

China's earliest way of counting years was using twelve symbolic animals to represent twelve years. They are (in order): rat, ox, tiger, rabbit, dragon, snake, horse, sheep, monkey, rooster, dog and pig. The year in which someone is born is called his "animal year." It is believed that these twelve animals can bring people good fortune, wealth and peace.

Sanniang Teaching Her Son

According to Chinese legend, there once was a man named Xue Guang who was a merchant always away on business. He had three wives who did not get along. One day the news came that Xue Guang had died. Soon after, his first and second wives married other men, leaving the third wife Wang Chun'e (called "Sanniang") and the old servant Xue Bao at home to bring up the first wife's son, Xue Yige. Yige grew up. When he found out that Chun'e was not his biological mother, he refused to listen to her. Chun'e became so angry that, as a warning to him, she broke her loom, the only source of income for the family. The lesson worked; from then on Yige studied even harder and eventually passed the imperial examination.

Longevity lock with the design of Sanniang teaching her son (front),
Qing Dynasty

Longevity lock with Sanniang teaching her son (back),
Qing Dynasty

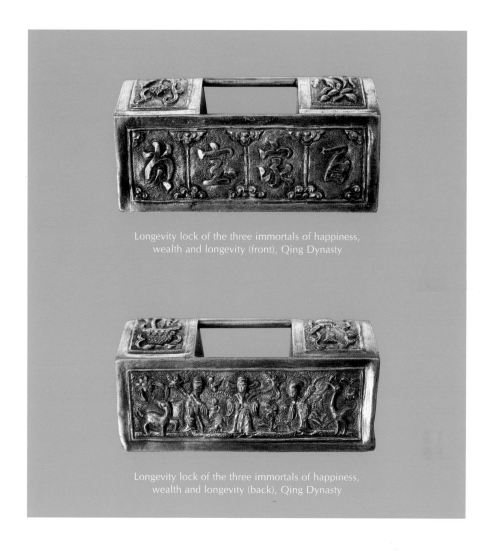

Longevity lock of the three immortals of happiness, wealth and longevity (front), Qing Dynasty

Longevity lock of the three immortals of happiness, wealth and longevity (back), Qing Dynasty

Three Immortals of Happiness, Wealth and Longevity

It's said that the Immortals of Happiness, Wealth and Longevity oversee, respectively, human misfortune and fortune, wealth and poverty, and death and lifespan. If a design with the three immortals is used in one's home, the family should be happy, wealthy and have long life.

Rectangular longevity lock, early 20th century

Octagonal lock with design
of a boy, Qing Dynasty

Eight-diagram-pattern longevity lock,
Qing Dynasty

Bucket-shaped silver lock,
Qing Dynasty

Hexagonal silver lock,
Qing Dynasty

Round silver locks, Qing Dynasty

Hexagonal silver locks,
Republic of China

Folk Silver Accessories

Round silver locks, Qing Dynasty

HAND ACCESSORIES

Hand Accessories

Silver hand accessories include bracelets and rings.

Bracelets

Bracelets appeared in the 2nd century BC, and became very popular in the 7th and 8th centuries; from the 13th to the 20th century, almost all Chinese women wore bracelets. The bracelets varied in materials and styles. The expensive materials included gold, silver or wood, while the complex techniques included plating, inlay, entwining and engraving, making the bracelets look extremely lavish.

Eight Treasures

The "Eight treasures" refer to eight Buddhist musical instruments: conch shell, Wheel of Law, precious umbrella, canopy, lotus, precious bottle, goldfish, and Endless Knot.

Hollowed-out silver bracelet with eight treasures and the character 寿, Qing Dynasty

Silver bracelet with peonies and vines, early 20th century

Peonies of Wealth

This design is composed of peonies, which are considered the queen of all flowers. Graceful and sumptuous, they represent auspiciousness and wealth.

Silver bracelet with designs of vines,
early 20th century

Vine-pattern silver bracelet,
early 20th century

Bracelet of twelve symbolic zodiac animals,
Republic of China

Bracelet of twelve symbolic zodiac animals,
Republic of China

Silver bracelet with designs of vines
and the eight immortals' eight treasures,
early 20th century

Hand Accessories

Flower-design, enamel-inlaid silver bracelet,
Qing Dynasty

Double-happiness silver bracelet,
Qing Dynasty

Enamel-inlaid silver bracelet with the
character 福, Qing Dynasty

Black agate and silver bracelet with two
dragons and a pearl, Qing Dynasty

Hollowed-out bracelet with
the character 寿, Qing Dynasty

Silver plaited bracelet,
Republic of China: Jiangsu

Silver bracelet, early 20th century

Black agate and sliver bracelet with
two dragons and a pearl, Qing Dynasty

Hand Accessories

Rings

Dating back over 2,000 years, rings were one of the most popular hand accessories; and their shape and style have not changed much since. A ring was generally decorated with engravings of auspicious words or creatures, inlaid with diamonds or precious stones, or sometimes small bells. There are rings made of several intertwined loops.

Qin, Chinese chess, calligraphy & painting

Frog Design

Nüwa (女娲) is the remote ancestor of the Chinese people. The word 娲 in her name is a homophone (*wa*) of 蛙 (frog) and 娃 (baby), frogs are thought to be beneficial and sacred creatures that bestow blessings on people, keeping their houses safe from disasters and bringing babies.

Silver rings of the Qing Dynasty

Enamel frog design

Frog design

Frog design

Frog design

Enamel frog design

Silver ring with dangling ornaments,
early 20th century

Chinese character福

Gem inlaid

Flower design

Chinese character 福

Enamel frog design
and three hooked loops

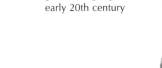

Four interlocked silver rings

Melon design

Hand Accessories

82

Chinese characters 福 and 禄

EAR ACCESSORIES

Ear Accessories

Earrings and Eardrops

Since about the 10th century, earrings have become popular among Han women in China. Until today, Chinese minority women of Achang and Li wear big hoops in their ears. Li women in Hainan Province wear hoops with a diameter reaching up to 18 cm, with each ear having more than 10 hoops of different sizes, forming a unique style.

The earliest eardrops found in China were a pair of 9-cm-long gold eardrops excavated from the Huata Ruins in Dingxian County, Hebei Province, dating back to the late 4th century. The major part of this pair of eardrops consists of gold cylinders, gold balls, gold flakes, and cones connected by a chain. Empress Xiaojing's (1565-1611) golden eardrops, unearthed from the Dingling Mausoleum in Beijing, are the most typical example of gold eardrops, depicting the legendary rabbit grinding herbs in the Palace of the Moon.

Dragon-design eardrops, early 20th century

Double-happiness eardrops,
Qing Dynasty: Beijing

Grape-design eardrops,
Qing Dynasty

Coral-inlaid earring,
Republic of China

Floral-basket-shaped eardrops,
early 20th century

Double-happiness eardrops, Qing Dynasty

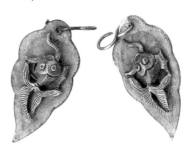

Eardrops with goldfish,
Qing Dynasty

Flower-design earrings, Qing Dynasty

WAIST ACCESSORIES

Waist Accessories

Waist accessories include jade belts, buckles and *diexie* belts.

Waist Pendants

The waist pendants are useful, decorative articles hanging around the waist. The Ancient Chinese liked to wear various waist pendants, including jade, fish-shaped decorations, perfume pouches, seals, or silver ornaments. Silver waist ornaments originated from articles for self-defense and daily use: small weapons or fire-lighting tools for men and sewing kits and other daily items for women.

In the Tang Dynasty (618-907), *diexie* belts, indicating ranks and titles, were compulsory ornaments for all civil and military officials. The *diexie* belts usually had seven articles attached, including a knife and a grindstone. This convention was abolished in 713, but belt accessories only grew more popular and even more diversified ever since. Silver items such as perfume pouch, fan case, glass box, seal, earpick, toothpick, knife, clamp, bodkin, tobacco pipe bag, jade- or coral-inlaid articles could all be seen on the belt. Some of these articles later developed into amulets.

Detail of the waist pendant with blessing-and-longevity design, Qing Dynasty

Waist pendants with blessing-and-
longevity design, Qing Dynasty

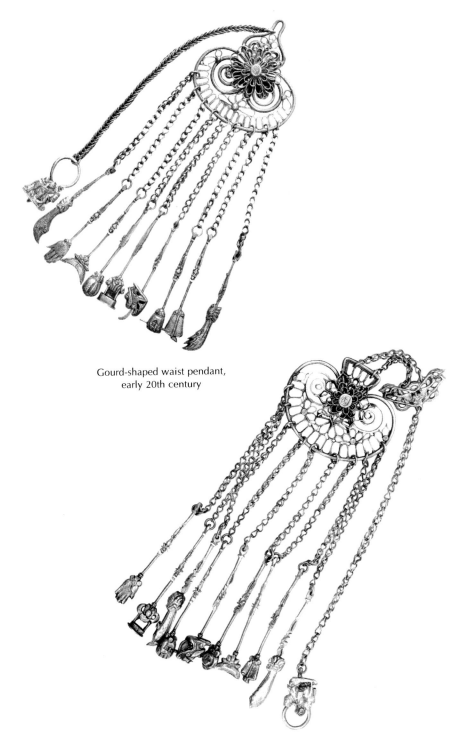

Gourd-shaped waist pendant,
early 20th century

Pouch-style waist ornament, Qing Dynasty

Waist pendants, early 20th century

Human-figure-design waist pendant,
Republic of China

Butterfly-shaped waist pendant, Qing Dynasty

Unexpected Good Fortune Befalling from Heaven

Spiders were considered as an auspicious insect by the ancient Chinese. They also believed that if one saw a group of spiders, it meant many good things would happen to him/her. The design of a spider lowering itself along a thread also represents impending happiness.

Floral-basket-shaped waist pendant with spider design, Qing Dynasty

Detail of the spider design waist pendant, Qing Dynasty

Butterfly-and-flower silver waist pendant, Qing Dynasty

Design of abacus and account book,
representing thrift, Qing Dynasty

Maodie Design

This design, also called "a cat playing with a butterfly," often has peonies which symbolize wealth. 猫 (cat) and 耄 (70 years old) are homophonic (*mao*), while 蝶 (butterfly) and 耋 (80 years old) are both pronounced *die*. Therefore, this design signifies wealth and longevity, and is commonly used on things presented to the elderly.

Waist pendant with a cat playing
with a butterfly, late Qing Dynasty

Mongolian waist-knife set, Republic of China

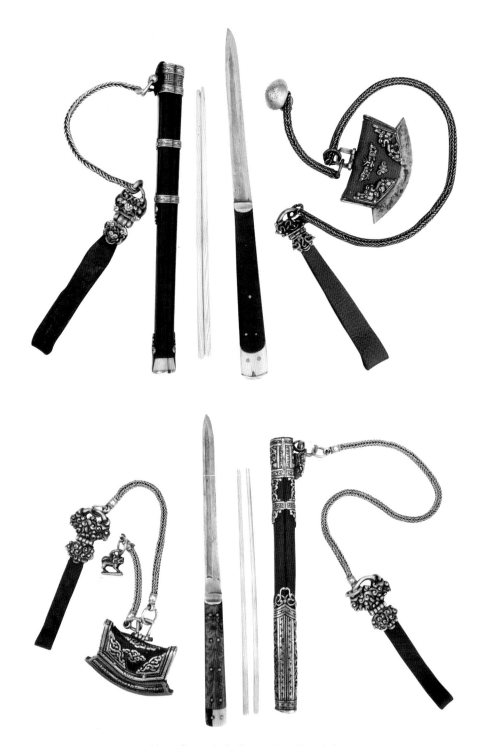

Mongolian waist-knife sets, Republic of China

Mongolian waist-knife ornaments,
Republic of China

Mongolian waist knife ornaments — flints, Republic of China

Waist Accessories

Silver sewing kits, Qing Dynasty

Auspicious silver items inlaid with animal tooth or horn,
Republic of China

Waist Accessories

Small enamel-inlaid pendants, late 19th century: Hebei

Fish-design pendants, Qing Dynasty

CLOTHING ORNAMENTS

Clothing Ornaments

The silver ornaments used on clothing include silver cap ornaments and silver buttons.

Cap Ornaments

These ornaments are generally used for celebrations of the birth of a child, and his/her first month and first-year birthday, in Shandong, Shanxi, Hebei and other areas in north China. The designs mostly are signs of blessing, high rank, longevity, peace and wealth. Elder women use designs like peony, chrysanthemum, spider, butterfly, crane and other things representing blessings, high position, longevity and happiness. Such are popular gifts given by daughter-in-laws to celebrate their mother-in-laws' birthdays.

Gilded cap ornaments,
late 19th century: Changzhi, Shanxi

Gilded cap ornaments, Republic of China: Shanxi

Buttons

An ancient clothing ornament, silver buttons are now rarely seen on Han people's clothes nowadays, but they are still widely used by Tibetans and Mongolians.

These buttons have various shapes and designs, such as hollowed-out, plum-blossom shape; hollowed-out with two dragons playing with a ball, blue with the character 喜, ingot, beast and chubby-baby, as well as fish, pomegranate and bat. People can choose different buttons according to their religious beliefs or preferences. For example, fish represents affluence; peach signify longevity; ingot implies wealth; lotus indicates uprightness; and chayote blessing and longevity.

Silver buttons, Qing Dynasty

There are usually five silver buttons on an outfit, but sometimes seven, nine, II, I3, or even more. They vary in sizes too. Some are as small as soybeans, weighing a few grams; while others are bigger than marbles, weighing tens of grams. These shining buttons add touches of luxury and elegance to clothing. Interestingly, they can also be used as currency when the owner is short of money.

Other than clothing, silver buttons can also be used on caskets for accessories or for the "four treasures of the study," as well as for exquisite books and painting scrolls.

Silver buttons with Chinese characters meaning "happiness as boundless as the East Sea," Republic of China: Shaanxi

Silver butterfly-and-flower buttons, Qing Dynasty

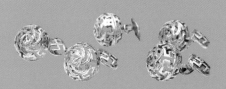

Silver hollowed-out buttons with "卐" (Buddhist symbol for auspiciousness), Qing Dynasty

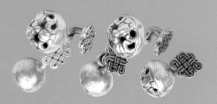

Silver hollowed-out buttons with Endless Knot design, Qing Dynasty

Silver buttons with the Buddhist "卐" symbol and flowers, Qing Dynasty

Silver buttons

Clothing Ornaments

Silver buttons shaped in a baby,
ingot, lotus, peach and flower, Qing Dynasty

HOUSEHOLD UTENSILS

Household Utensils

Silver household utensils, including bowls, basins, pots, plates, incense burners and wine bottles, were widely used by noble and imperial families. They have beautiful designs and delicate patterns.

Kneeling-goat kettle (for grinding an ink-stick),
faux-Qing-dynasty style: Shanxi

Enamel incense burner, Republic of China

Tripod incense burner (front), Republic of China: Hebei

Tripod incense burner (back), Republic of China: Hebei

Lotus-design vase,
Republic of China: Tianjin

Vase, faux-Song-dynasty style

Incense burner with longevity design, Qing Dynasty

Chinese chess-pieces holder with designs of *qin*, Chinese chess,
calligraphy and painting, Qing Dynasty

Silver pot, Republic of China

Silver wine pot, Republic of China: Shanxi

Gilded lotus-petal-design bowl, faux-Tang-dynasty style

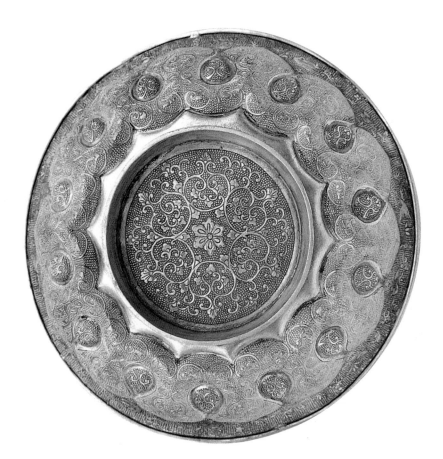

Bottom of the gilded lotus-petal bowl

122

Gilded wine cup, faux-Tang-dynasty style: Shaanxi

Gilded wine cup, faux-Tang-dynasty style: Shaanxi

Fruit plate with *ruyi* pattern, eight treasures and five bats surrounding
the character 寿 (front)

Bottom of the fruit plate

图书在版编目（CIP）数据

民间银饰：英文 / 王金华编著．

—北京：外文出版社，2008

（中国民间文化遗产）

ISBN 978-7-119-04676-1

I. 民... II. 王... III. 银—首饰—民间工艺—中国

—英文 IV.J526.1

中国版本图书馆 CIP 数据核字（2008）第 119617 号

出版策划：李振国

英文翻译：欧阳伟萍

英文审定：**May Yee** 韩清月

责任编辑：杨春燕

文案编辑：刘芳念

装帧设计：黎 红

印刷监制：韩少乙

本书由中国轻工业出版社授权出版

民间银饰

王金华 编著

© 2008 外文出版社

出版发行：

外文出版社出版（中国北京百万庄大街 24 号）

邮政编码：100037

网　　址：www.flp.com.cn

电　　话：008610-68320579（总编室）

008610-68995852（发行部）

008610-68327750（版权部）

制　　版：

北京维诺传媒文化有限公司

印　　刷：

北京外文印刷厂

开　　本：787mm×1092mm　1/16　印张：8.5

2008 年第 1 版第 1 次印刷

（英）

ISBN 978-7-119-04676-1

09800（平）

85-E-648 P